Superfoods

THE 101 BEST FOODS
TO LIVE LONGER AND
FEEL YOUNGER

Health Research Staff

Millwood Media LLC
Melrose, FL

Published by:

Millwood Media LLC
PO Box 1220
Melrose, FL 32666 USA

www.MillwoodMediaEpub.com

ISBN 13 : 978-1-937918-55-2

Health Disclaimer

Any and all information contained herein is not intended to take the place of medical advice from a health care professional. Any action taken based on these contents is at the sole discretion and sole liability of the reader.

Readers should always consult appropriate health professionals on any matter relating to their health and well being before taking any action of any kind concerning health related issues. Any information or opinions provided here or in any Millwood Media related articles, materials or information are believed to be accurate and sound, however Millwood Media assumes no liability for the use or misuse of information provided byMillwood Media.

No personnel or associates of Millwood Media will in any way be held responsible by any reader who fails to consult the appropriate health authorities with respect to their individual health care before acting on or using any information contained herein, and neither the author or publisher of any ofthis information will be held responsible for errors or omissions, or use or misuse of the information.

Table of Contents

Introduction

More than likely you have heard about super-foods, as the topic has received a good deal of attention in recent years. However, there is often some confusion as to what a superfood is or isn't. Much of that confusion stems from the fact that people hear the word "super" and assume that a super-food must somehow be very unusual, hard to eat or difficult to prepare. Yet, the fact is that most superfoods are foods you are already familiar with and have likely eaten before. The vast majority of superfoods are not at all "mysterious" or "strange," but are common foods that you already are familiar with, such as apples and spinach.

So exactly what are superfoods then? Superfoods are foods that are packed with nutrition or other health promoting benefits. In this regard not all foods are created equal, as some foods have enough nutrition in contrast to their calories to earn the title "superfood." As you will see throughout the course of this book, some superfoods are very unexpected and may even leave you a little surprised. Keep this fact in mind: superfoods are foods that can have a profound impact on your health, vitality, well-being and even your longevity. It is also important to keep in mind that not all superfoods work in the body in exactly the same way. Some superfoods made our list because they are nutrient dense while others, such as garlic, make the list because they are simply packed with helpful compounds that are likely to positively impact health.

Does this mean that you should only eat the 101 superfoods on this list? The answer to this question is of course not. Nature has provided us with an amazing variety of foods, and many foods that are not on our list are still worthwhile and good for you. Additionally, if you are on a special diet due to preexisting medical conditions, it is only prudent that you consult with your doctor regarding any changes that you make to your diet.

Keep in mind that this book isn't organized in a fashion where the first superfood that we selected is the most important and number 101 is the least important. Some foods will stand out for obvious reasons, but we are not selecting any one food as being the number one superfood you should eat. Instead it is important to remember that in order to be healthy, you need a balance of different foods. Wild Alaskan salmon might be great for you, but you shouldn't eat it for every meal. The 101 superfoods in this book need to be eaten in conjunction with one another in order to be healthy. So don't just pick ten and forget about the rest. And, of course, no one is expecting you to eat all 101 every week or even every month!

Finally, this book isn't intended to be a lengthy reference book. Many of these foods are such SUPER foods that an entire book could be written about each one. Rather the purpose is to provide a "pocket guide" that will familiarize you with the qualities of these superfoods as an encouragement to adding them to your grocery shopping.

By adopting and integrating these 101 superfoods into your diet (and replacing processed and fast foods) you will be doing wonders for your health. Improving your health so you will live longer and feel younger is what this book is all about.

* * * * *

Attention All Eagle Eyes: We've had a number of people proof this book before we released it to you, but there is a chance you might spot something that was missed. If you find a typo or other obvious error please send it to us. And if you're the first one to report it, we'll send you a free gift! Send to: **millwoodmedia@gmail.com**

* * * * *

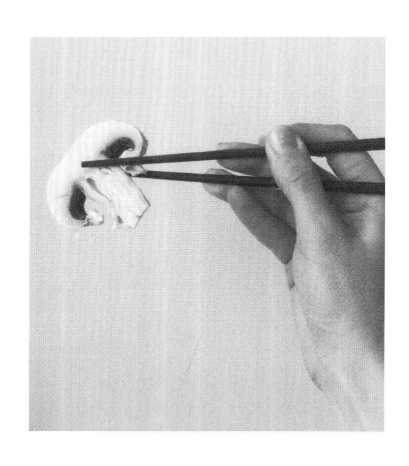

Superfoods

THE 101 BEST FOODS TO LIVE LONGER AND FEEL YOUNGER

ALMONDS

There are a lot of health benefits associated with almonds. Almonds are very high in vitamin E and protein as well as other nutrients such as magnesium and phosphorus. Almonds contain anti-cancer properties as well. Whether almonds are best raw or pasteurized is still a source of heated debate.

ALOE VERA

The aloe vera plant is best known as a treatment for burns, but aloe vera can do wonders when consumed as well. Aloe vera acts as a prebiotic helping the good bacteria in your digestive tract do their job.

APPLES

That's right, apples make the 101 superfoods list. Apples are full of nutrition, and there are many varieties to choose from, so you should never get bored. One additional reason that apples make our list is that the fiber in apples is very useful in helping the body remove toxins and unwanted materials.

APRICOTS

Almost everyone loves apricots, and that is a good thing, as apricots have anti-cancer properties. They also are high in vitamin C and iron and serve as a marvelous snack food.

ASPARAGUS

Asparagus is a very interesting entry for our top 101 superfoods. Fresh asparagus can be expensive in contrast to other vegetables, but it's worth it. Asparagus is high in numerous vitamins and minerals as well as iron and calcium. Many are surprised to learn that asparagus is even a good source of vitamin C. Further, Dr. Oz has listed asparagus as the top food to boost your sex drive.

AVOCADOS

Yes, avocados are loaded with fat. But when eaten in moderation, this is a welcome vegetable on our superfoods list. The fat in avocados is actually a very healthy fat. Further, researchers from Ohio State University have shown that avocados can boost the absorption of nutrients one receives from other fruits and vegetables. Considering that avocados taste great, there is nothing not to love.

BANANAS

Bananas are another superfood that might surprise many readers. Yet, there is no doubt that the banana earns a spot on our list of 101 superfoods thanks to its versatility. Bananas are high in a variety of B vitamins as well as vitamin C. They have a decent amount of protein and fiber and a variety of minerals as well. Bananas may not be "fancy," but they get the job done.

BARLEY

Barley is an impressive grain that is also made into flour. What helps make barley stand out is the fact that it is high in so many different vitamins and minerals, ranging from iron and magnesium to B vitamins, zinc and phosphorus. Loaded with protein and fiber, barley is a filling food that dieters will grow to love.

BASIL

You can depend on basil to liven up many different kinds of meals. This ancient spic continues to be a favorite around the world, and it is also one of the more healthy spices you can consume. Basil is low in calories, but packed with nutrition such as Vitamins A, C and high levels of vitamin K. Additionally, numerous B vitamins, calcium, iron, magnesium, zinc and manganese are just a few of the vitamins and minerals to be found in basil.

Beans

There are an amazing variety of beans, and they are all good for you. Beans are a low-calorie, high protein and nutrient packed way to boost the quality of almost any diet. What really helps beans stand out on our list is their versatility, as they can be used in so many different ways. The U.S. Department of Agriculture recently compared the antioxidant levels in over 100 foods. Three beans made the top four on the list, namely, kidney beans, pinto beans and small red beans.

Beef

Beef is a superfood? This all depends on what kind of beef we are talking about. Grass fed organic beef is high in iron and protein. Depending upon the cut, it can also be low in calories. Plus, this type of beef is also missing all the growth hormones and other problems so often associated with beef. For meat eaters, moderate servings of lean beef can be a smart choice.

Beets

When you look at the nutritional breakdown for beets, you might think that they don't compare well against foods like spinach. On a strictly nutritional level, this is true. However, this is not why beets make our list. Where beets really shine is in their ability to help protect the liver against disease.

Black Pepper

Surprisingly for some, black pepper is an aid in improving digestion. It's also high in antioxidants and is well tolerated by the body, meaning that you can enjoy its taste and receive health benefits all the time.

BLACK RASPBERRIES

Black raspberries are not the variety of raspberries that most people immediately think about. But black raspberries are special. They are closely related to red raspberries, but studies have shown that black raspberries contain powerful antioxidants. Researchers at Ohio State University recently found that black raspberries contain phytochemicals which can ward off skin cancer.

BLACKSTRAP MOLASSES

You might be surprised to see something as sweet as blackstrap molasses on the list. However, blackstrap molasses has a shocking amount of nutrition. High in iron, potassium, magnesium and trace minerals, blackstrap molasses makes for a great sweetener. Its nutritional makeup is enough to earn it a place in your kitchen.

BLACKBERRIES

Blackberries are high in a variety of vitamins and minerals and are quite high in antioxidants. It can be difficult to find blackberries fresh year round. However, frozen blackberries are usually available and can make for a fine addition to your cereal.

BLUEBERRIES

No superfood list would be complete without the addition of blueberries. In recent years, blueberries have received a great deal of attention and it is well deserved. Blueberries are amongst the highest of all fruits in antioxidants. This is especially true with wild blueberries. They also have anti-inflammatory and anti-cancer properties as well. Blueberries are one of the top superfoods you can eat, and you should try to work them into your diet at least a couple of times per week.

BROCCOLI

Not everyone likes broccoli. However, broccoli is so good for you that it is one of those foods you should eat no matter what. Broccoli is a nutritional powerhouse with lots of vitamins A, C and K and can also contribute to health in a variety of different ways. Various studies, including those by The Linus Pauling Institute, have found that the sulforaphane in broccoli can inhibit cancer.

BRUSSELS SPROUTS

It is no secret that many people hate brussels sprouts, and that is something of a minor tragedy. Brussels sprouts are not just full of vitamins and minerals like vitamins A, C, E and numerous B vitamins, but they are also an abundant source of anti-cancer compounds. In fact, Brussels sprouts can even work to repair your DNA!

BUCKWHEAT

Those looking for alternatives to wheat will love buckwheat. Buckwheat is unusual in several regards. First, buckwheat is not a form of wheat, despite its confusing name. However, buckwheat is a real gem of a food, as it is high in protein, amino acids, and antioxidants. Further, buckwheat is a good source of vitamins, minerals and fiber.

CABBAGE

What is most surprising about cabbage is that for only a few calories, it can provide most of your vitamin C requirement for an entire day. And red cabbage contains six to eight times as much vitamin C as green cabbage. In addition, you can expect cabbage to provide respectable levels of other vitamins and minerals as well.

CANTALOUPE

Cantaloupes give the body plenty of what it needs for very few calories. A rich source of antioxidants, cantaloupes also are high in both vitamin A and vitamin C. You can also count on cantaloupes for a surprisingly high level of protein.

CARROTS

What isn't there to love about carrots? Carrots are a great superfood for a variety of reasons. Carrots do not spoil easily, meaning that you can keep them for a long time. They work great for juicing and are packed with eye healthy vitamin A.

Cashews

The chances are good that you like cashews for their distinctive taste, but cashews are far more than a tasty treat. Cashews have a surprisingly high level of nutrition, as they are rich in protein, fiber, healthy fats as well as B vitamins and several minerals. In fact, you can expect to find high levels of iron, phosphorus, magnesium, zinc and manganese in cashews.

Cauliflower

Cauliflower is stuffed with an array of nutrition and has a large amount of vitamin C. Additionally, cauliflower is low in calories, but high in fiber and nutrition. Due to the fact that this veggie is very filling, it makes a great diet food. Cauliflower also contains the chemical indole-3-carbinol, which adds in DNA repair. The Journal of Nutrition recently published a study showing that compounds in cauliflower can assist with preventing breast cancer.

Cayenne Pepper

You may already love cayenne pepper, and the good news is that you should feel free to have more of this great superfood. Cayenne pepper does more than simply spice up your food, as it can help treat pain symptoms, inflammation and is high in vitamins and minerals.

CELERY SEEDS

You have likely never had celery seeds before, but this is one seed that you should consider adding to your diet. Celery seeds have impressive anti-inflammatory properties. In fact, celery seeds are even used in teas designed to treat inflammation. If you suffer from any form of inflammation, a teaspoon of celery seeds may provide you with some relief.

CHEESE

Cheese is a wonderful protein and calcium option for vegetarians. Low fat, organic cheese is a good source of protein and can help breathe a little life into otherwise bland dishes.

CHERRIES

On paper, cherries don't seem to have earned a place on our list of 101 superfoods, but cherries have a little secret. This superfood might not be a nutritional powerhouse, but it more than makes up for it in terms of fighting inflammation. Cherries have a powerful anti-inflammatory effect on the body. The University of Michigan Cardiovascular Center has stated that tart cherries can lower the risk of heart disease and diabetes.

CHICKEN

Lean, organic chicken is a great way to get your protein. Switching out high fat beef options with low fat chicken, turkey or fish selections is an easy way to keep the pounds off and your cholesterol levels low.

CHICKPEAS

Chickpeas have been popular for thousands of years. It's no real shock why. Not only do chickpeas star in many versatile dishes (take hummus, for example), but they are also nutrient dense. In fact, the nutritional breakdown of chickpeas is nothing short of impressive with a wide array of nutrition, protein and fiber. Odds are you can improve your diet just by adding one serving of chickpeas every week.

CHLORELLA

Health experts are often quick to tout the impressive properties of chlorella, and, to be sure, chlorella is a worthy addition to our 101 superfoods list. This tiny algae has earned so much attention for a variety of reasons. One major reason is that chlorella is very low in calories and yet high in protein and nutrition. How powerful is chlorella? It is believed that chlorella can improve the immune system and even protect against radiation exposure!

CINNAMON

Cinnamon has an undeniable taste that works well in so many foods. This is good news, as cinnamon is also one of the very best foods you can add to your diet. Cinnamon can help regulate blood sugar levels, it is extremely high in antioxidants and it is antibacterial. Since cinnamon is easy to buy and use, you might want to consider consuming a small amount everyday.

CLOVES

Cloves have been used since ancient times as a form of medicine. Cloves are very high in antioxidants, which is one of the principle reasons why this superfood is on our list.

COCOA POWDER

Cocoa powder is believed to be a very heart healthy food. Considering the fact that it's quite tasty, there is no real reason not to enjoy! Research is ongoing where cocoa powder is concerned, but all indicators are that it is good for both the heart and the brain. A study from the Proceedings of the National Academy of Science stated that the antioxidants in cocoa relax the blood vessels and can benefit the heart.For the most health benefit, look for all-natural sources of cocoa and avoid those with undesirable additives such as hydrogenated oils and high fructose corn syrup.

COLLARD GREENS

Green leafy vegetables, like collard greens, are the darlings of the superfood list. Like spinach and kale, collard greens are stuffed with nutrition. If you are looking for a change of pace and want plenty of vitamins A, C and K as well as calcium, then collard greens are a sure winner.

CRANBERRIES

Cranberries are loaded with nutritional and disease fighting goodness. Studies have shown that cranberries have anti-cancer effects and can also fight urinary tract infections. Further, cranberries and pure cranberry juice are low in calories as well.

DARK CHOCOLATE

Dark chocolate is a dangerous pick for our top 101 superfoods list, as there is plenty of room for error. In order to get the real health benefits from dark chocolate, you need to be careful about what type of chocolate you purchase, and you have to limit how much you eat because of the calories. However, with that stated, dark chocolate is a wonderful treat that has brain and heart benefits. For example, researchers at the University of Cologne have found that this type of chocolate can lower blood pressure. Just make sure you select dark chocolate that is high in cocoa and low in sugar.

EGGS

Eggs have received so much negative press in the past few years that many people still think that eggs are on the "don't eat" list, but this just isn't the case. Now no one is stating that you should eat ten eggs a day, but a few eggs a week is just fine. Eggs are a low calorie source of high quality protein and also contain the important brain nutrient choline.

Extra Virgin Olive Oil

Olive oil is full of brain and heart healthy fats, and it also serves as a great anti-inflammatory agent. It is important to keep in mind that the Mediterranean Diet that you likely have heard so much about has olive oil as one of its prime ingredients. So why choose extra virgin olive oil over regular olive oil? It contains even more antioxidants and heart-healthy benefits.

Fennel

Fennel is low in calories, but has a wide variety of nutrition in the form of vitamins and minerals. Fennel is also a good source of vitamin C and fiber as well. High in antioxidants, fennel is a great alternative when you feel that you need a change of pace in your diet.

Figs

On the days that you feel like you need to sweeten up your life a little bit, figs might be exactly the treat you desire. Figs are high in nutrition, such as potassium, and are being studied for the ability to fight cancer. The U.S. Department of Agriculture has given figs the thumbs up for their ability to help with weight loss. Best of all, figs are quite tasty.

FLAXSEEDS

Flaxseeds and flax oil are extremely high in omega-3 fatty acids, which are essential for brain and heart health. It is important to note that you need to grind flaxseeds in order to digest them properly. Yet, it is worth the trouble, as this is one of the best sources of omega-3 fatty acids around.

GARLIC

In a word, garlic is amazing. Garlic is so good for you that it almost sounds impossible. Throughout history, garlic has been viewed as something akin to medicine. Garlic has strong antibacterial, anti-viral, anti-fungal and anti-cancer properties. Yet, it is well tolerated by the body. Not only does garlic taste great, but also it is great for you.

GINGER

Ginger is one of the world's most loved and most used spices. Ginger is well tolerated by the body and has been used for thousands of years as an anti-inflammatory. Many people use ginger in the form of tea or consumed in soups and other dishes to tackle some of life's aches and pains. Further, ginger is routinely used to treat stomach conditions. Ginger may be useful for treating many other conditions as well, and research is ongoing.

GOJI BERRIES

Many health experts feel that goji berries are among the best foods that one can eat. When the Beijing Nutrition Research Institute analyzed the goji berry, they found these berries are simply loaded with vitamins, phytonutrients, and minerals. Further, goji berries have no less than 18 different amino acids, making this food a great source of protein. To be sure there are some exaggerations regarding the "miraculous healing abilities" of goji berries. But, in general, this is a very healthy fruit.

GRAPEFRUIT

Anyone who has ever been on a diet has more than likely had a grapefruit or two. A ripe grapefruit can actually seem more like a candy treat than a fruit, which makes it an easy addition to any diet. Grapefruits are also an excellent source of vitamin C. Phytonutrients in grapefruit called limonoids inhibit tumor formation and have also been shown to help fight cancers of the mouth, skin, lung, breast, stomach and colon.

GRAPES

Grapes may be common, but that doesn't detract from their ability to positively impact your health. Grapes actually have far more nutrition than people suspect, including good levels of vitamins C and K. Red grapes are also a source of the anti-aging flavonoid resveratrol, which has numerous health benefits.

GREEN TEA

If you research green tea online, you will soon discover that green tea is at the heart of countless studies and for very good reason. Green tea has powerful compounds that appear to fight against both cancer and aging. Considering that green tea has no calories, and that it actually helps boost your metabolism, this one is an easy recommendation. Just be certain that you are drinking real green tea and not a sugary, canned drink claiming to be green tea, as the market is full of those!

HEMP POWDER AND HEMP SEEDS

Hemp powder and hemp seeds are excellent forms of fiber and protein as well as vitamins and minerals such as zinc. What helps make hemp so unique is that hemp contains chlorophyll and essential fatty acids as well. This combines to make products such as hemp powder and hemp seeds true winners.

KALE

Kale is another leafy green powerhouse. Loaded with nutrition, kale is also loaded with anti-cancer compounds. Kale, along with broccoli and other brassica vegetables, contain a compound called indole-3-carbinol, which has been shown to help with DNA repair.

KEFIR

Wouldn't it be nice if there was a high protein, high calcium food that was also loaded with probiotics that would boost your immune system? That food does exist in the ancient form of kefir. Kefir has been viewed by cultures around the world as being vital to health for centuries and for good reason. Yogurt is also great, but kefir's probiotic characteristics make it even more impressive.

KIMCHI

You might be thinking "kimchi," really? However, there is no denying that kimchi is an interesting superfood. This fermented food, made from cabbage, garlic and other vegetables, is loaded with vitamins A, B, and C. It aids digestion, may prevent yeast infections and is viewed by many to be a powerful anti-cancer food.

KIWIS

These tiny fuzzy green wonders are not just tasty, but also very nutritious. One 50-calorie kiwi can give you all the vitamin C that you need for an entire day. If possible, keep a couple of kiwis in your refrigerator and eat them as soon as you think a cold might be coming on.

LEEKS

Leeks belong to the same family as garlic and onions, and, as a result, they share many of the same impressive properties of these other two superfoods. Leeks are high in B vitamins, vitamin C and vitamin K.

LENTILS

Lentils come in many different varieties but, in general, you can depend upon lentils to provide very high levels of protein, fiber as well as iron, folate and thiamine. However, it is important to note that while lentils are a fine protein source, they are lacking in some key amino acids. This is an important point for vegetarians to keep in mind.

LETTUCE

So what is it that is so special about lettuce anyway? The reason that lettuce makes the list as a superfood is that lettuce is extremely low in calories, yet very high in nutrition, especially in vitamins A and K. For these reasons, you should consider making lettuce one of your "go to foods."

MISO

Miso is a fermented product, often made of soybeans, that has been the subject of great study due to its health benefits. Miso can come in other forms, such as rice and even chickpea based, but soybean-based miso is still the most common. Among the many potential health benefits of miso is its ability to protect the body against radiation and prevent breast cancer.

MUSHROOMS
(BUTTON OR WHITE)

Your average, "common" mushroom is actually a pretty impressive little character. A small, low calorie serving of mushrooms can provide you with a good amount of several different B vitamins and proteins. Mushrooms are easily added to many dishes, and they also have vitamin D. The Agricultural Research Service has concluded that button mushrooms also boost the immune system.

(SHIITAKE)

In general, mushrooms are nutritious, high in protein and low in calories. However, mushrooms, like all the foods on our 101 superfoods list, have other health benefits in addition to their nutritional properties. Shiitakes are believed to have powerful anticancer properties that may help fight a variety of different cancers.

OATS

What food is easier to find than oats? Oats are available in virtually every grocery store. Yet, this simple food can work wonders in improving health. Oats can lower cholesterol levels, and can often be tolerated by those with gluten sensitivity issues. Oats are also heart healthy, thanks to high soluble fiber levels. In fact, the FDA has approved the claim that oats can reduce the risk of coronary heart disease. Oats are high in B vitamins, iron and magnesium. In short, oats are vastly superior to sugary breakfast cereals, so make the switch immediately.

ONIONS

Your average onion is the subject of a good deal of interest and research, as it is believed that onions may be able to contribute to human health in a variety of ways. Onions may fight cancer, heart disease, and the common cold. They also appear to have anti-inflammatory properties. Since onions are easy to store and use, this is one vegetable that is a great addition to any kitchen.

ORANGES

Oranges are easy to get and are usually available year-round. Combine these two facts with orange's high levels of vitamin C, and you have an easy pick for our superfoods list.The Commonwealth Scientific and Industrial Research Group of Australia reports studies that show oranges lower the risk of stroke and offer significant protection against some cancers.

OREGANO

Among the spices and herbs, oregano has made a name for itself. Clearly, this spice has long been used for its taste, but oregano is also a powerful disease fighter as well. Oregano has antibacterial and antiviral properties and is quite high in antioxidants. In fact, the US Department of Agriculture has stated that oregano has more antioxidants than any other herb! Oregano isn't just for your pizza or Italian meal. It's great on vegetables, eggs and omelets, cottage cheese and on and on.

PARSLEY

Parsley has become somewhat forgotten in recent years, as many people have come to see it as simply a decoration on their plates when they go out to eat. This is a shame! Parsley is, per-calorie, one of the most nutritious, commonly grown and continuously available foods in the world! If you want to get plenty of vitamin C and vitamin K, then this is the food for you. Parsley is also very high in iron and B vitamins as well. Plus, a recent University of Missouri study has found that a compound called apigenin, which is in high concentrations in parsley, can halt the growth of breast cancer cells.

Peaches

Peaches are very high in vitamin C, yet very low in calories. It also has high concentrations of lutein. Lutein gives the red, orange, and yellow colors to fruits and vegetables. This phytochemical may prevent heart disease, macular degeneration and cancer. It is this combination that earns this tasty fruit a spot in the top 101 superfoods.

Peanuts

Peanuts may not technically be nuts, as they are actually legumes. But that doesn't prevent them from making our list of 101 superfoods. Few foods on Earth have been shown to be as versatile as the humble peanut. Part of the reason that peanuts have become so popular and widely used is that they enjoy a wide nutritional spread. Peanuts are good sources of vitamin E, niacin, folate and manganese. They rival fruits as a source of antioxidants while also being a rich source of fiber and protein. Further, recent evidence shows that peanuts contain the compound resveratrol, which may have anti-aging effects.

Pecans

Pecans certainly get overshadowed by its better known nut rivals, such as walnuts, but this little nut really packs in the nutrition. Pecans have high levels of vitamin A, as well as respectable levels of vitamins C, E and K. Additionally, pecans have very high levels of manganese, magnesium, iron, zinc, phosphorus and several B vitamins.

PEARS

Pears may lack the vitamin C punch of many other fruits, but they make up for it with lots of insoluble fiber. Individuals looking for a tasty way to get more fiber in their diets will want to put pears on the list. Pears also have anti-inflammatory properties as well.

PEPPERMINT

Peppermint (the herb, not the candy) is easy to consume, especially in the form of peppermint tea, and it can greatly help with digestion. In fact, peppermint may even be useful in treating irritable bowel syndrome.

PRUNES

When it comes to fiber, many people think of prunes and prune juice. However, consuming prunes makes sense for another reason. Prunes are also quite high in antioxidants. Together this one-two punch of fiber and antioxidants serves to make prunes a winner.

PINEAPPLES

Pineapples are a special superfood. While they are packed with nutritional elements like vitamin C, this is not their only trick. A pineapple also has anti-inflammatory properties that can help your body recover from all sorts of muscle cramps and pulls.

POMEGRANATES

Pomegranates and pomegranate juice are high in antioxidants and are believed to help prevent a variety of diseases. The claims surrounding pomegranates are numerous and many are still unproven. But there is no doubt that pomegranates are loaded with nutrition. The journal Cancer Prevention Research recently published findings indicating that pomegranates can prevent breast cancer cells from growing.

PROBIOTICS

You might be thinking, "Wait a second… probiotics? That's not a food." This is technically true. While probiotics are found in yogurt, kefir and other foods, probiotics are generally more likely to be used in a supplement. However, they simply have to be included here due to their ability to improve the health of one's digestive tract. Keeping your digestive tract strong and healthy may prevent disease and makes the digestion of your food a little easier.

QUINOA

Quinoa (pronounced KEEN-wah) is an ancient grain that is gaining fast in popularity. This is due to the fact that it is high in fiber, protein, iron, vitamin E, zinc, magnesium and several forms of B vitamins, while also being low glycemic. Quinoa is an easy and tasty substitute for rice or potatoes and is also available as flour and flakes for baking applications.

RAISINS

You may remember raisins from your lunch box as a child. But hopefully, you haven't forgotten about these tiny dried grapes, as raisins are indeed a superfood. Raisins are high in antioxidants and are easy to store, making them a perfect and easy way to improve your diet. Raisins can also benefit your teeth. A study from The University of Chicago College of Dentistry showed that the phytochemicals in raisins inhibit mouth bacteria that lead to tooth decay.

RASPBERRIES

Yummy and delicious raspberries have become a mainstay in the world of desserts, and they also pack a healthy amount of nutrition. Raspberries are high in vitamin C and iron and have a good amount of fiber. However, the great strength of the raspberry perhaps lies in its high level of antioxidants. Further, raspberries also have anti-cancer properties.

ROOIBOS TEA

This dark red tea from South Africa is a great one for those looking for a caffeine-free drink. Rooibos is very high in antioxidants and is believed to have a host of protective benefits. The combination of zero caffeine and high levels of antioxidants is a good reason to work a cup of rooibos into your daily routine.

ROSEMARY

Rosemary isn't just for use in holiday occasion recipes. This ancient spice has a range of beneficial properties and may have a role in protecting the brain. Additionally, the exact same rosemary that you may have been eating your entire life also has anti-cancer and anti-inflammatory properties. Some research indicates that rosemary may also protect against tumors. *Fitness* magazine recently wrote about rosemary and mentioned that this herb can prevent gene mutations that could potentially lead to cancer.

SARDINES

Entire books have been written on how wonderful sardines are. The simple fact is that when it comes to low calorie, high quality protein, the simple, tiny sardine is tough, if not impossible, to beat. Since sardines are small fish and lower on the food chain, they don't accumulate the same levels of toxic metals, such as mercury, as larger fishes do. As a result, sardines are generally much healthier than larger fish. In terms of omega-3 fatty acids, sardines rank extremely well. Try opting for sardines with bones and you will get an added calcium boost as well.

SEAWEED

You name the seaweed, and the odds are that it is very good for you. Whether nori or kelp or any other seaweed, you can depend upon seaweed to be a low calorie, high protein food that is also loaded with vitamins and minerals. Seaweed expands in the stomach helping creating a sense of fullness.

Spinach

Leafy greens do very well on our list of 101 superfoods and with good reason. Spinach is almost like a self-contained vitamin of sorts, as it has numerous different vitamins and minerals. Spinach is just a great source of iron, its qualities include anti-inflammatory, anticancer, cardiovascular support, stress relief, maintains bone health and decreased risk of aggressive prostate cancer.

Spirulina

Spirulina has made its mark in the world of health and nutrition in a variety of ways. This cyanobacteria is a protein powerhouse that also contains important nutrients such as B vitamins. The "grocery list" of ways that spirulina may be beneficial to human health is impressively long as exemplified by the fact that spirulina may be able to inhibit the replication of the HIV virus.

Sprouts

Sprouts come in many different forms, ranging from beet sprouts to broccoli spouts, but what they all have in common is that they are nutrient dense. Since sprouts are very low in calories, but very high in nutrition, they are instantly welcome on our list of superfoods. Best of all, you can easily add them to salads.

STRAWBERRIES

The fact that strawberries taste great and are also great for you make them an easy pick for our superfoods list. However, it is important to note that non-organic strawberries are also usually loaded with pesticides, meaning that organic strawberries are the better pick. Plus, the USDA Agricultural Research Service found that organic strawberries have higher levels of antioxidants.

SUNFLOWER SEEDS

When you look at the nutritional breakdown of sunflower seeds, they almost look like a protein and fiber rich multi-vitamin. Sunflower seeds are very high in numerous nutrients, including Vitamin A and several B vitamins as well. Minerals such as iron, magnesium, manganese, zinc and phosphorus are all well represented. Sunflower seeds are truly a superfood.

SWEET POTATOES

If you are looking for a great side dish that is also very filling, then sweet potatoes will bring a smile to your face. These low-calorie, high fiber treats are also high in minerals and vitamins such as B vitamins and vitamin A. In particular, sweet potatoes rival carrots for their levels of vitamin A.

SWISS CHARD

Swiss chard is another leafy green that deserves your attention. Like collard greens, swiss chard is high in vitamins A, C and K and also stands out as a fine source of fiber.

THYME

In many households, the spice thyme is a forgotten player. However, thyme is certainly worthy of being on our list of the 101 superfoods. Thyme is believed to have antibacterial and anti-inflammation properties and is a great antioxidant and source of manganese.

TEMPEH

While tofu and soymilk, have various beneficial properties, tempeh is even more nutritious and easier to digest due to the fact that it is fermented. Tempeh has high levels of protein and fiber as well as iron, calcium, riboflavin, magnesium and potassium.

TOMATOES

Tomatoes are rich in antioxidants and, in particular, rich in lycopene. Lycopene is believed to have a powerful impact on different forms of cancer. Tomatoes can be consumed in many different ways and they still hold their nutrition even after they have been canned.

TUNA

Tuna is a wonderful seafood option, as it is very low in calories and very high in protein. However, tuna can also be high in mercury and other toxins. This is why it is important to exercise caution when buying tuna. Your best option is to consider canned tuna that is clearly marked as having been tested for low mercury.

TURKEY

Turkey (especially the white meat) is a low fat way of getting a good amount of protein and iron. When opting for organic turkey, it is also possible to bypass growth hormones and other problems frequently associated with non-organic animal products.

TURMERIC

The Indian spice turmeric is nothing short of amazing. Turmeric has been shown to fight cancer, improve brain function, have anti-inflammatory effects and may even have anti-aging properties. These are all good reasons to incorporate this tasty spice into dishes. It works particularly well as an ingredient in Indian food. However, for those that don't like the taste of turmeric, it is always available in pill form.

WALNUTS

It is difficult to overstate just how good walnuts are for you and how much they can contribute to your health. Your heart and brain needs omega-3 fatty acids, which walnuts are loaded with. The U.S Department of Agriculture Human Nutrition Research Center has shown that walnuts can benefit cognition and slow the aging process. Walnuts are easy to eat and widely available. Further, walnut butter works perfectly well on toast in the morning.

WATER

Yes, you did read that correctly, water. Most people don't drink enough water, and to make a long story short, your body really, really doesn't like this. Dehydration is more common than people realize, and it can even make you look older! One smart move is to invest in a water purification system. Even a cheap one is better than nothing. Most water supplies have traces of everything from bacteria to heavy metals.

WHEATGRASS

Many claims get tossed around where wheatgrass is concerned, but there is no denying that wheat grass is low in calories and absolutely packed with nutrition. Per calorie, wheatgrass is high in protein, vitamin A, vitamin E and potassium. You name the issue, and someone has claimed that wheatgrass can treat it or even cure it. While it is true that people do get carried away with their wheatgrass claims, this food's nutritional density is definitely high.

WHITE TEA

Many of the benefits of green tea can also be found in white tea, but there is one important distinction. White tea has only a fraction of the caffeine of green tea, making it a perfect choice for later in the day or for those who feel that they already have too much caffeine in their diets.

WHOLE WHEAT

One of the healthiest moves that many people can make in their diets is to switch to whole wheat breads and grains. In contrast, "white" bread is essentially devoid of nutrition. Yet, a word of caution is necessary. Just because a bread or cereal states that it is "wheat" doesn't mean it is a nutritional powerhouse. It is necessary to read the labels of wheat products carefully, as ingredients such as high fructose corn syrup and other undesirable ingredients are frequently added to the mix and should be avoided.

WILD ALASKAN SALMON

The topic of salmon can be a confusing one. People often hear, "Eat salmon" and think that all types of salmon are created equal. Salmon are typically large fish and, as a result, they tend to have higher levels of mercury and other heavy metals. However, this is not the case with wild Alaskan salmon. As is true with sardines, wild Alaskan salmon have high levels of heart and brain-healthy omega-3. Farm raised salmon should be avoided due to the levels of pollution.

XYLITOL

You might be unfamiliar with the sweetener xylitol, which is derived from tree bark, but it deserves a place on our 101 superfoods list. There are many good reasons to switch out your sugar with xylitol. For example, xylitol has been clinically shown to actually fight tooth decay! Xylitol works to kill off bad bacteria in the mouth and thus prevent tooth decay. Xylitol is also low in calories and low on the glycemic index.

YAMS

Yams are low in calories, but high in nutrition. Further, yams are low on the glycemic index, meaning that you won't have blood sugar spikes after eating them. This tasty food is also quite filling and makes an excellent side dish.

YOGURT

Along with kefir, yogurt stands out amongst dairy products for its high calcium and high protein levels. Yogurt also has the added benefit of probiotics that the body needs for a healthy immune system and digestive tract.

CLOSING THOUGHTS

If you noticed there were 102 foods, instead of the 101 advertised, you're right. We threw in a bonus food to make two points. First, many different types of health "bonuses" will come to you if these foods form the core of your daily diet.

Secondly, there certainly are many more deserving foods that didn't make the list. The vast majority of the foods we chose are easy to find, easy to use and are available in your local grocery or health food store.

In general, when possible, you should consider organic options, especially for your fruits and vegetables, as this will allow you to avoid pesticides.

By incorporating these 101 superfoods into your diet, you will quickly see an improvement in both how you feel and how you look!

HANDY LIST
SHOPPING FOR THE
101 BEST SUPERFOODS

FRESH PRODUCE

Apples

Apricots

Asparagus

Avocados

Bananas

Basil

Beans

Beets

Black Raspberries

Blackberries

Blueberries

Broccoli

Brussels Sprouts

Cabbage

Cantaloupe

Carrots

Cauliflower

Celery Seeds

Cherries

Collard Greens

Cranberries

Fennel

Figs

Garlic

Ginger

Grapefruit

Grapes

Kale

Kiwis

Leeks

Lettuce

Mushrooms *(Button,*

White, Shiitake)

Onions

Oranges

Oregano

Parsley

Peaches

Pears

Pineapples

Pomegranates

Prunes

Raspberries

Rosemary

Spinach

Sprouts

Strawberries

Sweet Potatoes

Swiss Chard

Thyme

Tomatoes

Wheatgrass

Yams

NUTS, SPICES, BAKING

Almonds

Cashews

Pecans

Peanuts

Sunflower Seeds

Walnuts

Raisins

Extra Virgin Olive Oil

Black Pepper

Blackstrap Molasses

Cayenne Pepper

Cinnamon

Cloves

Peppermint

Turmeric

Cocoa Powder

Dark Chocolate

MEAT, DAIRY

Beef

Chicken

Tuna

Turkey

Wild Alaskan Salmon

Cheese

Eggs

Yogurt

CANNED GOODS

Sardines

Chickpeas

Lentils *(dried)*

Tuna

Wild Alaskan Salmon

TEA

Green Tea

White Tea

WATER AISLE

Water

CEREAL

Barley

Whole Oats

HEALTH FOOD SECTION/STORE

Aloe Vera

Buckwheat

Chlorella

Flaxseeds

Goji Berries

Hemp Powder and Hemp Seeds

Kefir

Rooibos Tea *(or Red African Tea)*

Miso

Probiotics

Quinoa

Seaweed

Spirulina

Tempeh

Whole Wheat

Xylitol

DELI/MAKE YOURSELF

Kimchi

Chicken

Turkey

WHEN A "SUPERFOOD" IS NOT A SUPERFOOD!

There are a number of different foods and supplements that have been promoted as superfoods, when if fact there is no scientific basis for such a claim. One such example is the acai berry, which has been widely promoted as a superfood that has many different amazing health benefits. But the truth about the acai berry is much more modest. Here is information provided by the National Center for Complementary and Alternative Medicine (NCCAM) and is a good example why you should always confirm any outrageous claims you see about a so-called "superfood."

ACAI

This fact sheet provides basic information about acai (pronounced ah-sigh-EE) – common names, uses, potential side effects, and resources for more information. The acai palm tree, native to tropical Central and South America, produces a reddish-purple berry that is related to the blueberry and cranberry. The acai berry's name, which comes from a language of the native people of the region, means "fruit that cries."

Common Names: acai, açaí, Amazonian palm berry
Latin Name: Euterpeoleracea

What It Is Used For

- Acai has become popular in the United States, where it has been promoted as a "superfood." Acai berry products have been widely marketed for weight-loss and anti-aging purposes, but there is no definitive scientific evidence to support these claims.

- The acai berry has long been an important food source for indigenous peoples of the Amazon region, who also use acai for a variety of health-related purposes.

- Acai fruit pulp has been used experimentally as an oral contrast agent for magnetic resonance imaging (MRI) of the gastrointestinal tract.

How It Is Used

Acai berry products are available as juices, powders, tablets, and capsules.

What the Science Says

- There is no definitive scientific evidence based on studies in humans to support the use of acai berry for any health-related purpose.

- No independent studies have been published in peer-reviewed journals that substantiate claims that acai supplements alone promote rapid weight loss. Researchers who investigated the safety profile of an acai-fortified juice in animals observed that there were no body weight changes in rats given the juice compared with controls.

- Laboratory studies have focused on acai berry's potential antioxidant properties (antioxidants are substances that are thought to protect cells from damaging effects of chemical reactions with oxygen). Laboratory studies also have shown that acai berries demonstrate anti-cancer and anti-inflammatory activity.

Side Effects and Cautions

- There is little reliable information about the safety of acai as a supplement. It is widely consumed as an edible fruit or as a juice.

- People who are allergic to acai or to plants in the Arecaceae (palm) family should not consume acai.

- Consuming acai might affect MRI test results. If you use acai products and are scheduled for an MRI, check with your health care provider.

- Tell all your health care providers about any complementary and alternative practices you use. Give them a full picture of what you do to manage your health. This will help ensure coordinated and safe care. For tips about talking with your health care providers about CAM, see NCCAM's Time to Talk campaign at nccam.nih. gov/timetotalk/.

Sources

Acai. Natural Medicines Comprehensive Database Web site. Accessed at naturaldatabase.com on April 19, 2011.

Acai (Euterpeoleracea).Natural Standard Database Web site. Accessed at naturalstandard.com/ on April 19, 2011.

Acai berry diet. Natural Standard Database Web site. Accessed at naturalstandard.com on April 19, 2011.

Marcason W. What is the açaí berry and are there health benefits? Journal of the American Dietetic Association. 2009;109(11):1968.

Schreckinger ME, Lotton J, Lila MA, et al. Berries from South America: a comprehensive review on chemistry, health potential, and commercialization. Journal of Medicinal Food. 2010;13(2):233-246.

For More Information

Visit the NCCAM Web site at nccam.nih.gov and view "Using Dietary Supplements Wisely" (nccam.nih.gov/health/supplements/wiseuse.htm).

BONUS INFORMATION

7 DAYS TO SUPER ENERGY

Contents

INTRODUCTION

It is one of the ironies of modern life that at a time when medical advances allow us to overcome so many of the problems that were once thought of as incurable and the technology is available to make all our lives so much easier, life in reality has never been more difficult!

This is reflected in so many different ways, some minor but many far less so meaning that for millions of people all over the world, just getting through the day feels like it's a major achievement.

There are of course many reasons why this can happen as life does not always treat us the way we would like it to, but one common complaint nowadays is that people often feel that they have a lack of energy, not enough 'get up and go' to successfully navigate through whatever their daily routine throws in their direction.

And although health, fitness and wellness is now a huge online business – it is for example generally agreed that 'weight loss' information is the second most searched for subject on the net – there is surprisingly little information about energy and more specifically, about how you can increase your energy levels.

In fact, what you are going to read in this book could literally change your life because once you know how to increase the levels of energy available to you, then it becomes far easier to ensure that you never again find yourself in a 'place' where you feel permanently tired and drained of energy no matter what you seem to do.

There is one thing to appreciate before we start however.

The reason that this book focuses on a 7 day program is that replacing energy that has apparently trickled away over the years is not something that is going to happen overnight because there are no 'quick fixes'. In fact, the very things that most people would probably think of as being capable of supplying a quick 'energy burst' will often leave you feeling more tired than ever.

At the same time, this does not mean that it is going to take a full 7 days to feel any benefits. As soon as you start making the appropriate changes that you are going to read here, you are likely to begin to feel increasingly energetic pretty quickly but of course, every person is different.

Nevertheless, if a lack of energy is a big problem, what you are about to read could be life changing.

WHAT'S THE PROBLEM?

When researching this book, one thing that became clear very quickly was that there are many different reasons why an individual might feel tired or fatigued.

However, one commonality of the majority of people who are asking questions on the net (and using other resources like magazines and newspapers) about why they feel almost permanently tired is the fact that most of these people are trying to live a healthy life. Which is exactly the kind of life that suggests that a lack of energy should not be a problem for them.

And yet, they are suffering, so it does not appear that living in a healthy way is good enough to stave off fatigue and tiredness on its own. It is therefore necessary to examine what other contributory factors there might be as it will no doubt help you to combat fatigue if you can establish why you feel so tired and listless in the first place.

Some of the factors that serve to reduce the energy available to power your body through the day, or to limit your body's ability to use the available energy efficiently, are as follows:

A lack of sleep:

It should be fairly obvious that if you do not get enough sleep every night, you are inevitably going to feel fatigued and listless throughout the following day. In addition however, there is also an unfortunate cumulative effect if you are not getting enough sleep. In this case, it is fairly inevitable that the fatigue you feel every day will gradually increase as the energy deficit takes an ever-increasing toll on your capacity to perform at the top of your game.

Stress:

Stress is something that is almost unavoidable in the fast paced modern world we live in but this does not mean that it is either acceptable or unavoidable. Stress can never be acceptable because it is a condition that is often at the root of a very wide range of medical problems (both physical and psychological). On top of this, it does not have to be something that you accept either, as you will discover later in the book.

Even so, it is the fact of 21st-century life that stress hits most of us at some time or other (for some people, it is everyday) and it is therefore essential to understand that stress is going to make you feel far less energetic than you might otherwise be several reasons.

Firstly, if you have ever gone to bed immediately after a big argument, you will already be aware that when your brain is still hot-wired after such a quarrel, it is impossible to go to sleep quickly. You are still stressed, you nerves are on edge and the adrenaline is still pumping, so the chances of getting to sleep in this mental state are fairly minimal.

Secondly, being stressed makes your body less efficient while the nervous energy that we would normally associate with being tense and stressed is energy that is being leached from more positive usage. When you are uptight and stressed, your body is producing large amounts of hormones, a process which in itself uses up a significant amount of the energy that you would otherwise have available to help you through the day.

This is why being stressed and uptight is likely to leave you feeling drained and shattered immediately afterwards as the energy high that has been driving your highly excited state quickly falls away.

Nutrient deficient food:

The fact that our modern diet is responsible for an ever-expanding range of health problems (or perhaps more accurately, deficiencies) might come as a surprise to some people.

After all, they see an increasingly growing choice of seemingly delicious, nutritious foods on the shelves in the local hypermarket or store, a lot of which is increasingly affordable, so they quite naturally assume that our modern diet should provide all of the goodness and nutrients that we need.

Unfortunately, however, nothing could be further from the truth for many different reasons.

Firstly, the fact that people want (or maybe need) the price of the weekly food shopping to keep falling puts a great deal of pressure on commercial food manufacturers to increase efficiency and output levels.

Consequently, the quality of food products that you buy is almost incessantly falling as a direct result of wanting to pay less for bananas and/or beefsteak than you were paying before.

As an example, imagine that you are planning to purchase a commercially produced fruit pie. If you want that pie to contain only top quality, highly nutritious fruit and other materials, then the price you will have to pay will reflect the quality of the content of the product.

If however you want to pay a rock bottom price, then quite obviously, the quality of content will also be reflected in the price, meaning that the fruit included is nowhere near as nutritious or healthy as it could have been.

Even with something as humble as a simple fruit pie, there is however a chain of production and at every stage of that chain, economies have to be made and shortcuts need to be taken as well.

For instance, the farmer who grew that fruit is being pushed by the pie manufacturer (do not even begin to call them bakers!) to produce increasingly cheap fruit for his pies. This means that the farmer has to produce more than before to keep his business afloat.

Consequently, he (or she) turns to chemical fertilizers and insecticides to make sure that the business is capable of producing a maximum amount of produce from every square meter of land that is being farmed.

However you want to cut it, there are no safe chemical fertilizers or insecticides. Not only do these chemicals pollute the environment while altering the pH balance of the soil so that it becomes increasingly infertile and toxic, they destroy the healthy microorganisms in the soil which is basically where the goodness in the food you eat should come from.

Furthermore, chemicals take varying amounts of time to break down, with some becoming increasingly toxic as they do so. These poisons can stay in the soil (which is going to be growing even more fruit or other crops next year) and in the water supply (the same water that you may be drinking right now) for many years to come.

There are other problems too. While every amateur gardener understands that insects can be a nuisance when you're trying to grow any kind of plant, it is still a fact that only about 6% of species of insects carry any kind of threat.

Unfortunately, chemical insecticides are entirely indiscriminate, meaning that they kill both the good and bad insects, which is becoming an increasing concern for scientists who are seeing the balance of nature being indelibly shifted.

These chemicals can even creep into the meat element of your diet as cows and sheep graze on pasture under which the soil has been damaged by many years of chemical ministration. Other creatures such as pigs and chickens are given feed that is likely to be tainted in the same way.

Improperly prepared foods:

Another factor that you need to take into account when looking at the genuine value of your diet is the fact that whether you are eating at home or in a restaurant, the chances are that the food preparation methods you (or the chef) use are designed more for convenience than they are for retaining the nutrients that exist in the food being prepared.

For instance, whenever you boil vegetables, you remove a significant percentage of the nutrients from them which are then tipped away with the water after you have finished cooking. Instead of boiling vegetables, it therefore makes a great deal more sense in nutritional terms to steam them so that they retain the goodness as steam leaches far less of the available nutrients than does surrounding them with boiling water.

Frying food is not a particularly good option either as doing so adds extra fat to your food, which is not really something you want to do. A quick sauté in a healthy unsaturated oil such as extra virgin olive oil may not be too bad, but frying food for several minutes in a less healthy oil all but guarantees that your food absorbs a percentage of that oil, which is very bad for your all-round health.

Another thing to appreciate when considering the nutrients in your food is that some nutrients (or a lack of them) have been directly linked to fatigue and listlessness.

For example, to quote from the Home Health UK site, "The main types of anemia are caused by shortages of iron, vitamin B12 and folic acid, all of which are needed to produce red blood cells."

Anemia is a condition that is most commonly seen in pregnant women or those who suffer an unusually heavy monthly cycle, but if you are anemic for any reason and these nutrients are missing from your food, it could be a major cause of a constant feeling of being tired.

Drugs by the 'back door':

There is another extremely important consideration when it comes to meat products, something that very few people are actively aware of.

In many developed Western countries, it is increasingly common for commercial farmers to feed drugs to their livestock to make sure that the creatures they are breeding for meat gain the maximum amount of weight possible and that they stay disease-free.

The additional weight being ladled on to these poor animals is almost completely water, meaning that an increasingly large percentage of your meat-shopping bill is buying you nothing more than plain water!

The fact is, farm animals are increasingly pumped full of (or fed) drugs such as antibiotics, hormones and steroids in an effort to keep them disease-free, maximize their weight and so on.

As a result, if you eat meat products without really knowing what is in them, the chances are that you are consuming an unknown amount of unidentified antibiotics and other drugs without even knowing it.

Nowadays, it is a recognized fact that the citizens of most developed Western countries are far too over-reliant on antibiotic drugs, primarily because for several decades, the first choice of most doctors when confronted with a sick patient has been to prescribe this particular form of drug.

Although doctors all over the world are happy to prescribe antibiotics for a wide range of conditions (although there is some evidence that this may be becoming less common) including such things as influenza, these drugs are in fact only effective against bacteria, whereas influenza is caused by a virus, meaning that antibiotics will make no difference whatsoever.

However, because antibiotics have been so rashly overused for such an extended period of time and because bacteria mutate on a regular basis, there are now many strains of bacteria that are entirely resistant to most or all antibiotic drugs. MRSA, the so-called 'flesh-eating bug' is just one example of a highly drug-resistant strain of the extremely common staphylococcus aureus bacteria.

The bottom line here is, irrespective of how careful you are about not taking antibiotic drugs unless it is absolutely necessary, you could inadvertently be ingesting antibiotics and other potentially harmful drugs every time you sit down to the dinner table.

The problem that you must therefore understand is that while you might be trying to eat a healthy diet that is theoretically capable of providing all of the energy you need, it does not follow that because all the food on the table appears to be nutritious that it really is. Consequently, it is a fact that many people who suffer a lack of energy every day could be victims of the 'tricks' of the food production industry.

And of course, if this is the case, the chemicals and drugs that you are taking could be exacerbating the problems that leave you feeling listless and fatigued because of problems like stress and a lack of sleep.

Western medicine:

As highlighted in the previous section, it is now widely accepted that for many decades, people have been far too willing to take a huge cocktail of prescription drugs that were given to them by their doctor or medical care professional, usually on the basis that 'doctors always know best'.

And while there is no doubt that in the majority of cases, the drugs prescribed were entirely appropriate to the condition being treated, this has not always been the case.

Hence, you may have built up an internal residue of chemicals over the years that are at least partially responsible for your general feeling of ennui.

Furthermore, because Western medicine focuses on dealing with the symptoms of illness and disease rather than on getting to the root cause of the problem before dealing with it at that level, many conditions that people suffer from never leave them or allow them to return to or retain 100% good health. This lack of conditioning can be seen in many different ways, with a constant feeling of being tired one of the most common.

Your environment:

The environment that surrounds you every day is likely to have a very significant effect on your general state of health and wellness as well for a wide variety of reasons.

For example, while air-pollution is perhaps not as endemic as it was 50 years ago, it is still a major problem if you happen to live in a large town or major city. If you're surrounded by motor vehicles every day, the vast majority are still pumping out poisonous carbon monoxide fumes, which naturally means that you are breathing these potentially noxious substances every day.

Furthermore, while there are millions of people all over the world who might be termed 'sun worshippers', having the sun beating down on the top of your head every day is not always a good thing. There are many side-effects and potential illnesses associated with too much sunshine (e.g. skin cancer).

On the other hand, everyone needs sunshine on their skin from time to time because without it, you have no chance of creating vitamin D (which is produced by the effects of the sun on your skin), which is in turn responsible for regulating the ability of your body to absorb and use calcium efficiently. If your body is not using minerals and trace elements properly, this is extremely likely to contribute to your general feeling of tiredness.

There are also people who suffer a recognized form of depression known as Seasonal Affective Disorder that strikes people in the depths of winter when sunlight is at a premium. One of the most commonly reported effects of this condition is a lack of energy and a general disinterest in life, something that passes for 99% of sufferers once the spring arrives and the sun appears over the horizon once again.

Where you live, what season it is and everything that surrounds you can therefore have a significant role to play in dictating how much energy you have available.

Your physical condition:

I would suggest that it should be pretty obvious to most people that if you are badly out of shape, you are inevitably going to feel as if you lack energy and the 'get up and go' to do something about remedying the situation.

However, the fact that more than 60% of the adult population of the USA is either overweight or obese (a percentage which is exploding) tends to suggest that my assumption may not be completely accurate!

It is nevertheless a fact that if you are overweight or obese and you do not do any exercise, then without making significant lifestyle changes, your lack of energy is a problem that is never likely to be remedied.

While carrying too much weight does not guarantee that you will lack energy per se (some of the most successful bodybuilders carry more weight than they should, but it is 'good' muscle weight), for the majority who have a weight problem, a lack of energy is pretty much a given byproduct of their condition.

101 combinations:

The reasons that I have put forward for why you might suffer from a lack of energy so far could suggest that there is going to be one reason or another that you can readily identify that is entirely responsible for your condition.

However, the fact is that in the majority of cases, it will be a combination of circumstances or reasons which are causing the way you feel and not all of these reasons might be apparent or included in this list, mainly because every person who feels tired does so for different reasons (and more often than not because of a combination of them).

For instance, if you are stressed, then it is likely that you're not sleeping very well and that you are probably not concentrating on eating a healthy diet quite as much as you should be. Hence, there are three factors that between them are causing you to feel the way you do, although it is probable that in this situation, one problem is leading to the others.

Nevertheless, if you understand that a problem like a lack of energy is likely to be caused by a combination of factors, the way that you deal with the situation should become that much clearer.

BEGIN AT THE BEGINNING

Although the previous chapter is designed to help you identify some of the factors that might have a part to play in dictating how drained you feel every day, it is important to understand that these are only intended to be a general guidelines to get you started and definitely not a detailed medical opinion.

However, if you do suffer from a lack of energy that blights your life every day, perhaps the most important thing to do is find out exactly why you feel the way you do. And there is no sense in guessing here because you have to establish whether there is any specific reason why you feel the way you do before you can concentrate on increasing your energy levels in a more general, all round way.

In other words, the first thing that you should do if you feel that you lack energy or that each day is becoming increasingly difficult to get through is make an appointment with your doctor or other medical care professional to seek their advice to establish whether there is any genuine underlying medical condition causing you problems.

If you feel okay but would just like to become more energetic, then it it's probably not necessary to seek the doctor's advice but if on the other hand you feel constantly tired, there may be a specific medical reason for the condition that needs to be identified before deciding upon the most effective form of remedy.

For instance, it was highlighted earlier that the main causes of anemia include a lack of iron, folic acid and vitamins B12. If you therefore have an anemia problem that is making you feel constantly tired, remedying the situation may involve nothing more complex than introducing more foods that are rich in these nutrients to your diet or using supplements to make sure that you have sufficient iron and vitamins to overcome the problem.

If you genuinely feel that you consistently lack energy, having a word with your doctor seems to make a good deal of sense. At least in this way, you will either isolate the underlying problem so that it can be dealt with, or put your mind at rest that there is no such problem in the first place.

IT'S ABOUT YOUR LIFESTYLE

Assuming that there is no underlying medical condition causing your lack of energy, you have arrived at the beginning of your seven-day program to increase your energy levels. This is the point from where you have to identify why you think you feel as if you lack energy because if you don't do this, you cannot begin to make the necessary lifestyle changes that will see you rectifying the problem.

For instance, if you are a person who is always stressed, you probably have a major cause of your lack of energy pinned down already. A similar situation is likely to apply if you are badly out of shape or overweight, so you cannot realistically expect to be super-energetic.

You therefore need to start thinking about how you go about remedying the situation that is causing you to suffer a lack of energy before going any further. This is important because while this book is focused on increasing your energy levels over a relatively short period of time, if you have to make large-scale lifestyle changes, it is likely to take a little more time before you feel the biggest benefits of making these changes.

For example, despite advertisements for commercial diet products that claim you can drop 10 lbs. or one clothes size per week, this is not going to happen for most people and even for those who do achieve success, the weight loss is almost entirely because they shed water. Moreover, weight lost in this way never stays away for the long term, so you need to think about this particular aspect of your program to increase energy levels in more depth.

In short, if you have obvious factors that are going to limit the likelihood of you feeling full of beans, energetic and vital every day, you must include specific measures to combat these limiting factors in your own seven-day energy increase program. If this is losing weight or reducing the amount of stress that you consciously feel, then you may want to focus on some aspects of what you are going to read in this book more than on others.

However, whatever the reason is that you are currently

lacking in energy, you will find a solution to your problem in the following chapters which will deal with your lack of energy in both a physical and psychological manner.

THE PHYSICAL SIDE OF GETTING MORE ENERGY

It is an oft-bandied cliché that is nevertheless true that you are what you eat. In short, the physical 'you' that you see staring back at you from the mirror in the morning is the sum total of every morsel of food and every liquid ounce of fluid you have ever consumed, which, taken to its logical conclusion, should tell you one thing.

If you don't have the energy that you think you should have, then the food and drink that you have consumed thus far has not been capable of providing that energy for one reason or another. What you therefore need to do is start making dietary changes that will turn the picture around so that in the future, the 'you' that stares back in the morning is made up of a very different 'mix' to what you are made of now.

There are two ways that you should approach this problem, doing so in a macro-manner and also by managing your dietary intake on a micro-level as well.

Exactly what this means will become clearer as you continue reading, but your starting point is to view your daily food and drink consumption on a macro-basis by considering your diet as a whole.

MACRO-MANAGING YOUR DIET

If you are what you eat and you don't have enough energy, then your diet and lifestyle is either not providing the energy or not enabling you to release it as efficiently as you should. You therefore need to start making changes but before doing so, there is another vital factor to appreciate.

The evolution of mankind is a relatively slow thing, which means that to all intents and purposes, our bodies and more importantly our metabolisms are still pretty much the way they were 1000 years ago. Sure, there have been some changes as we have (for example) gradually become taller, but the fact is that our internal 'workings' have not changed a great deal.

However, our daily diet has changed by a massive amount, perhaps far more than you might ever have imagined. For example, before the turn of the 20th century (in 1890), the average US citizen consumed 5 lbs. of sugar a year, the figure is now 135 lbs. per annum, and that is up from 26 lbs. a little over 20 years ago!

Furthermore, as the diet of most citizens of developed nations has become increasingly focused on processed and convenience foods, our consumption of processed white flour, meat products of no determinable origin and the like have also skyrocketed.

The results of these dietary changes have unfortunately been overwhelmingly negative in a huge number of different ways, most of which do us no favors. And the starting point for all these negative effects is the fact that the human digestive system has not adapted quickly enough to accept these changes and still be as efficient as it should be.

What this means is that for most of us, our digestion is struggling to process the food that we feed into our system every day and while our digestive tract does a remarkably good job everything considered, it is unfortunately fighting a battle that it can never win.

As a result of these changes, your gut or colon has gradually built up a store of toxic and noxious substances over the years that your digestive system does not have the ability to push through. Most of these substances come from your diet, with others contributed by the environment (from the air you breathe), medical drugs and so on.

As these materials congregate in your colon, it naturally becomes less effective which in turn means that the buildup rate of toxic substances accelerates. It's a classic vicious circle because the more accumulated rubbish there is, the less efficient your system becomes, so even more is acquired. Perhaps not surprisingly, all of this toxic material buildup inevitably slows you down and reduces your energy levels.

For instance, many millions of people in the USA, UK, Australia, Canada and the like regularly suffer constipation and/or diarrhea which are both classic signs that your colon is not in tiptop condition.

Although to some people these symptoms are indicative of a recognized medical condition (e.g. Irritable Bowel Syndrome), for most it is highlighting the fact that you are not feeding your digestive system the foods and nutrients it needs. And while constipation and/or diarrhea might be unpleasant but no more, you should understand that they could indicate that you are more susceptible to far more serious medical problems such as colon cancer, which is one of the biggest killers in the Western world.

In short, your digestive system, colon and bowel are clogged up with toxic materials that are draining your energy in more ways than one.

For instance, you could be eating the most nutritious foods in the world but if your digestive system does not have the capability of processing them to extract all the nutrients, you are naturally enough not getting all of the benefits. There is therefore an immediate loss of energy and health here.

This is further exacerbated by the fact that because your digestive system is packed with toxic materials, your body expends a significant amount of energy keeping the worst effects of these toxins in check.

This is energy that your body is 'stealing' from you in an effort to keep you healthy but it is nevertheless energy that you do not have access to.

To put this into some kind of perspective, a healthy colon should weigh around 4 lbs. whereas some autopsy reports carried out on individuals who clearly lived a

less than healthy life reported a 40 lb. colo...
would this have added a significant extra com...
to any weight problems these individuals suffere...
clear that their digestive system would have been all...
incapable of doing its job.

When it comes to macro-managing your diet, there
are therefore several considerations to take into account.

The first thing that you must do if you want to increase
your energy levels is to reduce the level of toxins (and
other 'nasties' like parasites) that are currently putting a
significant drain on your energy resources.

To do this, you might choose a commercially produced
colon-cleansing product, but this is not necessary, nor
does it make a great deal of sense either when compared
to natural dietary changes that will do the same thing.

The beauty of adopting a natural approach to getting
rid of this accumulated junk from your colon and bowels
is that by doing so, you make changes that will help to
minimize the future buildup of these toxic materials as
well. Getting rid of this accumulated toxic mélange in a
natural manner and making sure that it doesn't return is
one of the easiest and most effective ways of improving
your energy levels.

Now, I am not going to pretend that you can remove
this toxic mix from your body immediately, because it
has taken years to accumulate so it is going to take a little
time to shift it.

Even so, the changes take weeks rather than years and

benefits within days because
our system to rejuvenate itself
:xtract the maximum amount
the foods you consume.

ok at exactly what you should
e consuming if you want to
increase your energy levels as quickly as possible.

THE DIETARY DON'TS...

As suggested, the average citizen of most Western countries consumes a massive amount of processed sugar, which is just about the worst thing you can do for many different reasons. Some of these reasons are directly related to decreased energy levels, whereas others are more related to medical or physical problems that excessive sugar might cause which can also lead to low energy.

Most people probably understand that sucrose or processed white sugar is essentially pure energy, so they might therefore imagine that if you feel that your energy levels are low, eating sugar rich foods like candies, cookies, cakes and the like should be the perfect answer.

Unfortunately, this is the exact opposite of the truth because while a sugar rich food (or a soft drink which is how most people consume the majority of their daily sugar intake) will give you an immediate 'sugar high', it will also increase insulin levels that will bring you down again just as quickly.

Sadly, many people find that after coming down from the sugar rush, they are even less energized and more tired than they were before, explaining exactly why consuming processed sugar is a transitory and relatively ineffective energy booster.

The potential problems caused by overconsumption of processed sugar do not however stop here. For example, most people are aware that vitamin C is an essential nutrient for continued good health but they may not be aware that one of the purposes it serves is to reduce the chances of cancer cells developing.

Unfortunately however, to do this, vitamin C must gain access to the white blood cells that combat cancer, and in this respect, they are in competition with sugar cells. Consequently, the more sugar you take on board, the less efficient vitamin C is able to be at preventing cancerous cells developing.

There is also evidence that too much sugar damages your immune system's ability to control your body efficiently and as it is believed that 80% of your immune system is focused on your digestion (where all the toxic rubbish is, remember?), it should be clear that processed sugar is not a healthy source of energy by any stretch of the imagination.

In a similar way, all other processed foods tend to have had most of the nutrients stripped from them. Sadly, the levels of more harmful substances like saturated fats (in burgers for example) have usually not been reduced whereas additional sugar has been introduced to enhance the flavor.

Once again, eating processed foods is not going to help to increase your energy levels, instead helping to pile up more of the toxic mountain lodged in your digestive tract that slows you down and steals your energy.

The bottom line here is, if you eat a diet that is rich in processed foods, sugar, saturated fats and the like, you are only encouraging the development of the noxious energy drain lodged in your digestive tract.

Do this and you cannot realistically hope to increase your energy levels, so don't do it. There is also the question of piling on the extra pounds to be considered as well, because most overweight people (apart from those with a clinical reason for their condition) know that it is a processed food diet that is most likely to make it ever more difficult to get into their clothes.

WHAT YOU SHOULD DO

Okay, now we have looked at the 'don't' side of a diet that will help to increase your energy levels, let us consider what you should be doing.

The first thing that you must do is drink lots of fresh water. The minimum recommended water intake for everyone is at least eight glasses a day but as long as you don't go crazy, drinking more than this is a good idea, particularly during this first week when you're trying to get the energy boost ball rolling.

Note that this is specifically water you should be drinking (preferably alkaline water) and not other caffeine rich drinks like coffee or tea. Although some people find that caffeine gives them a boost, it is always a temporary one that needs replenishing on a regular basis, hence the idea of having a 'coffee' habit. In similar way to a sugar rush, coming down from a caffeine-high can also reduce your energy levels still further, so try to drink water as opposed to anything else. If you want to "liven" up the water some, squeeze a lemon or a lime into it and pack it with ice.

One alternative beverage that you might include, especially in the early days when you are trying to detoxify your system, is green tea, as it is believed that the polyphenols in green tea help to detoxify your body as well as playing a hand in preventing diseases such as liver complaints and diabetes. There is plenty of evidence that green tea is good for you in many ways, so including three or four cups of green tea in your new dietary regime every day would help to clear out your system, thereby increasing your energy levels.

To get started with your 'clean out', buy a good stock of organic fruits and vegetables that can be eaten raw. The idea of this is that for the first two or three days, the only foods that you should consume are raw fruits and vegetables to get your system 'kickstarted'.

As these organic products are high in the nutrients, vitamins and trace minerals that your system has been missing, you should find that within this 48 to 72 hour period, you already start to feel the benefits of this lifestyle change. At the same time however, you should not overdo things by eating too much as the idea is that you minimize the strain on your digestive system while feeding it all the natural nutrients that help to normalize the balance in your colon and bowels.

To help take this one stage further, you should also include probiotic supplements in your new diet for this first week as these are the 'good' bacteria without which your digestive and immune system are immeasurably weakened. As a result of the buildup of toxic garbage in your gut, the balance between good and bad bacteria has significantly shifted in favor of the latter harmful variety, you need to start to redress the balance by feeding your system probiotic bacteria.

Incidentally, there are plenty of sites on the net where you can buy probiotic supplements, so all you need to do is run a standard Google search to find somewhere suitable, or go to your local health food store as they will have them too.

Next, you should add psyllium seeds or husks to your diet as well as flax seeds as the first of these helps to neutralize the toxic effects of the buildup of waste as well as loosen the built up materials, whereas flax seeds absorb moisture while expanding in your colon, thereby helping to remove noxious substances and toxins.

Another substance that is often recommended as part of a short-term detoxification diet is bentonite in liquid, powder or tablet form. This is a type of edible clay that acts as a bulk laxative that forms a gel after absorbing water in your gut. As it does so, it also absorbs many of the toxic materials that you're trying to shift, thereby accelerating the cleansing process.

If you stick to your 'raw veggie' fast for two or three days while taking the supplements shown, you should find that you feel a noticeable difference after you have finished.

And while there is no particular harm in continuing to use the probiotics, seeds and bentonite tablets for a short period of time to optimize the internal cleansing process, you should not do so over the longer term. If you were to do this, your system may come to depend upon these 'artificial stimulants' for good health, which is not something that you want to encourage.

However, fast for two or three days using only raw organic foods while also following this colon cleansing process and you will feel far more energetic and vital than you have felt in a long time.

WHERE TO NEXT?

After you have cleaned out your system and you are feeling better than you have felt in months (or perhaps even years), I would guess that you do not want to go back to the situation where even getting out of bed in the morning seemed like a major task.

If not, you cannot afford to go back to your old dietary habits either because as the results of your 'clean out' should have made obvious, it was those dietary habits that made you feel listless, fatigue and drained at the end of every day.

What you must therefore do is adopt a healthy balanced diet rather than going back to the 'bad old days', perhaps by following the guidelines on the page at www.choosemyplate.gov

As you can see, the two largest groups of foodstuffs that you should be consuming are the fruits and vegetables on the left, while meat products, grains and dairy on the right-hand side are far less prominent.

However, you should also make sure that when you constructing a healthy balanced diet based on the information provided on the webpage highlighted earlier, you should do so using the most nutritious alternatives possible.

For example, a significant percentage of the grain

products that you eat should be whole grains such as brown rice, whereas as suggested earlier, the most nutritious vegetables and fruits are almost always the organic variety. Moreover, if you are including meat in your diet, it would be best to look for organic but also non-antibiotic treated meat products.

Sure, there is no doubt that if you buy the best quality food available, you will have to pay a little more but in the long run, it may even work out cheaper. If for example you can save a few hundred dollars on medical bills every year because you (and perhaps your family) are healthier than you have ever been, then the extra outlay on better quality foods is more than justified.

One final factor to bear in mind is that it is your brain that controls how energetic you feel. Consequently, making sure that you include plenty of brain friendly foods in your diet, the kind of things that will help to keep your brain in tiptop condition such as oily fish like mackerel, salmon and sardines (which are all rich in Omega-3 essential oils) plus plenty of dark, leafy vegetables is a very good choice.

MICRO-MANAGING YOUR DIET

The idea behind micro-managing your diet is that even for people who would not necessarily agree that they are energy deficient all of the time, it may happen sometimes.

For instance, there are certain times of the day when you really need lots of energy, while other times, energy is far less essential. It therefore makes sense to feed your body with as much energy as it needs at the times when it most needs it, rather than doing so at times when energy is far less essential.

It is for this reason that many nutritional experts suggest that the most important meal of the day is breakfast, because a healthy, hearty breakfast sets you up for the day and provides you with the energy you need to get going. At the same time, most people who work a full-time job also need energy in the afternoon as well, so a reasonable lunch is also essential.

At the end of the day however, energy is far less important because after you have dealt with the rigors of the day, your body naturally starts to slow down as bedtime approaches. This is therefore the time of the day when the smallest amount of energy is needed.

And yet, most people grab an apple as they charge out of the door in the morning, race through lunch before eating a big dinner when they get home.

In other words, in terms of providing the necessary energy to keep you going, what you are doing is completely the wrong way round if this is what you do.

A healthy balanced breakfast provides you with the energy you need to get over or through what is usually the hardest part of the day, while following this with a balanced lunch should be sufficient to provide your body with the energy you need to get through the afternoon as well.

It is however a fact that some people feel an almost overwhelming urge to have a nap in the afternoon, and unfortunately, if you are at the office or factory, this fact does not make this 'I need a nap' feeling go away.

Nowadays, there are some more enlightened companies who are beginning to recognize this fact. They have accepted that allowing employees to have a 15 to 20 minute nap is far better than having a drowsy employee who is incapable of achieving anything for an hour or two, but these organizations are not yet in the majority, and they probably never will be.

Hence, what you should do is eat a lunch that is designed to prevent you from feeling sleepy afterwards. To do this, try to avoid carbohydrates at lunchtime, focusing instead on a lunch that is predominantly green vegetable and protein-based.

This works because proteins are broken down in your digestive system into amino acids, one of which is tyrosine which is known to keep you sharp and alert. Hence, instead of a carbohydrate packed lunch (which releases serotonin into your brain, a hormone that relaxes you), aim to eat something that is protein rich such as a tuna and boiled egg salad or steamed fish and vegetables.

Another idea that is very popular (but not scientifically proven) is that some herbal supplements can help to overcome a temporary energy deficit, with many people swearing by garlic capsules or tablets, gingko biloba or ginseng.

The fact that all of these 100% natural substances seem to be capable of reviving energy levels without reverting to potentially harmful substances like processed sugar and are convenient to carry and take, makes this another option that you might like to consider.

WHAT'S THE ROOT OF THE PROBLEM?

As I highlighted at the beginning of the book, your psychological state can play a very significant role in dictating how energetic you feel. If for example you are under constant stress, it is far harder to maintain a positive attitude and without a positive attitude, most people would find it very difficult to be energetic and enthusiastic.

Hence, you need to decide whether there is a psychological reason why you don't feel as if you have any energy, starting with the obvious 'suspects' such as stress and a lack of sleep.

If you cannot sleep, it may because you are stressed, but if you haven't had any sleep for a couple of days, it becomes far more likely that you will feel stressed as your temper and general demeanor suffers.

You therefore need to identify what is the root cause of your problem, because if you can do this, then it becomes relatively easy to deal with.

For example, it might seem almost too blindingly obvious but the reason why people sometimes cannot sleep is because the bedroom is not as dark as it should be. Even though this might sound like a relatively minor thing, it is in truth anything but because if there is too much light, it interferes with your brain's ability to handle melatonin secretion which is the hormone that is responsible for your body clock.

From this it follows that the darker your bedroom is, the more relaxed your sleep is likely to be which in turn guarantees that you will wake up in the morning completely revitalized and full of energy. This is one reason why some people wear eye-shades in bed as it ensures that they get the full eight hours of uninterrupted sleep which most people need to remain energetic and enthusiastic.

As mentioned before, foods that are rich in carbohydrates release serotonin, which helps to relax and calm you down, so carbohydrate rich foods form an ideal pre-bedtime snack (in moderation). Some people also find that a warm bath, perhaps with an infusion of aromatic oils helps to calm and relax them before bed too, so this is something else that you could try if a lack of sleep seems to be causing energy problems during the day.

DEALING WITH STRESS

Stress is a terribly debilitating condition, one that literally drains you of the very last drop of energy and vitality, as well as playing an active role in causing many potentially fatal conditions such as heart attacks and strokes. Hence, while fighting against stress to combat the lack of energy that you feel is important, it is probably not the most important reason for doing so.

The basic idea behind most strategies for combating stress is that stress comes about because a situation or scenario prompts you to be psychologically unhappy or uncomfortable. It is often characterized as being the modern version of the 'fight or flight' reaction to danger or a threat that would have been understood by our caveman forbears.

This in turn means that if you could teach yourself or somehow learn to react to external stimuli in a more positive way, then stress and the negative effects it has on your psychological (and ultimately physical) well-being would be minimized or banished forever.

In essence therefore, dealing with stress is something that you have to learn, and there are several widely recognized ways of doing so.

The first strategy that you might consider using for dealing with stress is by using hypnotherapy, the medical version of hypnotism.

While there is still a good degree of mystery attached to why hypnotism works in the way it does, it is generally believed that when someone is in a hypnotic trance, the hypnotist or hypnotherapist who has induced that trance is able to communicate directly with the hypnotized subjects subconscious mind.

The relevance of this is that by the time you reach adulthood, the way you react to specific situations is almost always a subconscious reaction, something that you don't even think about.

To understand this concept better, think of it this way: a newborn baby is a blank canvas as he or she has learned literally nothing about the world. Thus, if an axe-wielding madman were to charge headlong at this newborn character, they would probably stare at this wild-eyed onrushing figure with mild bemusement.

In contrast, you and I would prepare to fight or (more likely) run away because this is a conditioned reaction that we have learned over the years, and conditioned reactions come from the subconscious mind.

Therefore, because a hypnotherapist has the ability to communicate directly with your subconscious, they can analyze why you react in a stressed way to certain situations and conditions before changing your beliefs and reactions by communicating directly with the root cause of them.

Many people over the years have found that hypnosis or hypnotherapy is extremely effective for dealing with a wide range of subconscious reflex reactions such as minimizing the worst effects of stress because hypnotherapy has the ability to remove the trigger that prompts the reaction.

Consequently, if you are a person who suffers stress that seems to be draining all of your energy, this is definitely an option to investigate.

Hypnotherapists are generally located in cities of

100,000 or more so one should be available to most of the population.

An alternative that you might want to consider is to investigate the idea of self-hypnosis or using hypnosis products that you can buy on the net.

Although you may be a little skeptical when first introduced the concept of self-hypnosis, there are lots of websites where there is plenty of information about it and more importantly, about how successful it can be.

For example, there are detailed, step-by-step instructions about how you can hypnotize yourself at wikiHow, while there is lots of free information available for download on the SelfHypnosis.com site.

Alternatively, try running a search for 'hypnosis products', because there are many sites where you can buy hypnosis audios, CDs, videos, books and everything you could think of that could be associated with hypnosis.

The basic idea of hypnosis as a way of dealing with stress is that through mastering your subconscious reactions, you learn how to relax instead of reacting in a stressed manner.

A similar thing can be associated with another strategy that many people use to conquer their tendency to react in a stressed manner, which is to use yoga together with the associated practices of meditation and deep breathing to learn to overcome their susceptibility to stress.

Once again, if you are a person who suffers stress and you therefore find that your general levels of energy are not as good as they could be, this is another option which you can either learn from others in a controlled environment or start the ball rolling in the comfort of your own home via the medium of the net.

Again, it really doesn't matter where you live, there will be yoga classes reasonably close to most.

The other way of doing things is to start learning yoga from the net from any one of a number of sites that are focused on both the physical and the mental side of learning about this ancient Eastern practice.

The basic idea of yoga is that by learning to control the way your mind reacts to situations and circumstances, you can achieve a far higher level of relaxation than you have previously managed. Consequently, as there is such a focus on mind control associated with yoga (primarily through meditation), it is an ideal pastime for anyone who suffers a lack of energy caused by reacting in a stressed manner to external stimuli.

The basic exercises attached to yoga are characterized by participants striking stationary poses that are designed to improve muscle flexibility and strength. These poses are known as asanas and they range in difficulty from being relatively easy to very hard.

Hence it is important that if you would like to start investigating whether yoga is for you from home, you should use a site where the degree of difficulty is noted so that you do not attempt something that may cause physical damage or injury.

As far as the spiritual side of yoga is concerned, there are many different types of meditation associated with different forms of yoga, most of which came from different religions. There are also resources like meditation CDs as well as meditation supplies which can help you to meditate successfully.

The final thing that is intrinsically linked to yoga is having the ability to breathe deeply and slowly on demand because once you can do this, you have the capacity to take control of even the most stress inducing situation by forcing yourself to breathe properly.

The importance of this can be demonstrated by the fact that most people in a stressful situation will breathe quickly and shallowly, which immediately limits the supply of oxygen to the brain and to the body. This in turn makes a situation that was already becoming difficult considerably more so.

In this scenario, by starving your brain of oxygen, you have naturally limited your capacity to make well-reasoned, logical decisions, hence rapid breathing always exacerbates an already stressful situation.

Almost everyone who learns the art of deep breathing reports that as part of the learning process, they acquire the ability to be conscious of when stress is starting to happen and the fact that their breath is becoming quicker and more shallow at the same time. Once they acquire this level of consciousness, it becomes far easier to control their breathing, thereby bringing stress under control as well.

As there is with meditation, there are many different ways of learning deep breathing but using the Pavlov method is one that you should definitely consider because it is again focused on conditioning your subconscious mind which as established earlier is where stress comes from.

If you can use any of these methods to successfully conquer your susceptibility to stress, you are immediately going to see a marked improvement in your energy levels as far less of your energy is wasted on futile stressful situations that you could nor previously control.

And of course, it should go without saying that as a part of your seven-day program to increase your energy levels, the sooner you start to control the stress you feel, the quicker you are going to start enjoying increased energy.

THE IMPORTANCE OF EXERCISE

One of the ironies of feeling that you have no energy is that fact that it discourages you from taking regular exercise.

However, commencing a program of regular exercise is probably one of the best things you can do in terms of boosting your energy levels because the fact that exercise burns energy makes your body far more efficient at processing energy in the future.

Viewed from the opposite angle, if you do not do exercise of some description, you are encouraging your body to be an inefficient machine for processing energy, which it will more than gladly do.

But when you don't allow this to happen (i.e. when you exercise at least four times a week), your body gradually becomes fitter, healthier and a far more efficient energy processing plant, which of course means that if you exercise in this way on a regular basis, you will naturally feel more energetic, lively and vital.

What you really need is four sessions of cardiovascular or aerobic exercise every week as a minimum, something that works your heart, lungs, leg and arm muscles so that your whole body gets a workout.

Now, we are not talking about being an Olympic athlete here, nor am I suggesting that you go from doing no exercise whatsoever to trying to run a half marathon.

Indeed, starting off with something as simple as 15 minutes of brisk walking every day is a good idea because it is essential that you start off slowly and gradually build up, rather than going crazy from the beginning which is highly likely to cause injury.

Of course, the exercise program that you instigate will be dictated by your age and present physical condition, but you must nevertheless understand that if you want to feel more energetic and lively, taking up cardiovascular exercise is possibly the most important factor of them all.

Exercise encourages your metabolism to speed up so that all of the energy from the food you consume is channeled in the right directions is an example of why this is so.

At the same time, the fact that cardiovascular exercise involves movement will help every other process you have learned in this book to be more effective than it would otherwise be.

For instance, even something as simple as walking prompts your digestive system to become more efficient because you are using the muscles of your upper legs, hips and buttocks, all of which are adjacent to the muscles that control your lower digestive system. Furthermore, it is an acknowledged fact that regular exercise improves oxygen flow to all of the organs of your body, including your brain, which helps to combat stress and tension.

Indeed, many people who take regular exercise report that doing so is one of the most effective ways of combating stress as it allows them to dissipate their aggression as they run, swim or cycle and it is natural that regular exercise will help you sleep better as well.

As suggested, if you haven't exercised for some time, start off slowly with 15 minutes of brisk walking, if possible every day but failing this at least four times in your first week. Then, add another 5 minutes in the second week, another 10 minutes in the third week and so on until you can comfortably walk for an hour at a brisk pace.

Other options that are very good are cycling and swimming, with the latter being ideal for those who are a little older or perhaps not so strong because swimming uses every muscle in the body while there is no 'impact' (with the attendant risk of injury) as there would be if you were pounding the streets jogging 5 miles every evening.

In reality, as long as you are doing sufficient aerobic exercise, your energy levels will rapidly increase, especially if you combine this with anaerobic exercise by practicing yoga. You could for example practice yoga three times a week in combination with aerobic exercise four times every week so that you have a complete exercise program that is almost guaranteed to skyrocket your energy levels pretty much irrespective of whatever else you decide to do.

Conclusion

As you have read, there are lots of strategies that you can adopt that help combat a general feeling of listlessness or a specific feeling of tiredness and fatigue that comes over you at a particular time of the day.

Nevertheless, because most people who suffer from a lack of energy do so because of a combination of factors rather than any single thing that drains the energy out of them, I would suggest that you adopt the same approach to reversing the situation.

For example, if you start your organic fruit and vegetable fast tomorrow while combining it with the supplements that will help to clean out your system, it would also make sense to start looking into the viability of hypnotherapy or yoga and take your first 15 minute walk as soon as you have finished reading these final few paragraphs.

And as highlighted, do not underestimate the power of exercise to re-energize your body and your mind.

Walking or jogging when combined with yoga and even something as simple as stretching makes sure that your brain is getting the oxygen it needs to manage your body efficiently.

In combination with cleaning your body out at the same time, even the gentlest exercise makes it far easier for energy to be channeled in the most beneficial directions, so you will naturally feel re-energized remarkably quickly.

But you are not going to get anywhere if you don't take action, and while I appreciate that taking action is possibly one of the last things you might want to do if you have no energy, you also know that without action, nothing is ever going to change.

You now have the tools you need to do the job. It is up to you to use them.

So get going to a new life of super energy!

Made in the USA
Lexington, KY
10 May 2013